BUBBLES in the Bathroom

Discover the fascinating science in everyday Life

Susan Martineau

Published by b small publishing ltd.,
The Book Shed, 36 Leyborne Park, Kew, Surrey, TW9 3HA, UK

© b small publishing ltd. 2008

1 2 3 4 5

Design: Louise Millar   Editorial: Susan Martineau   Production: Madeleine Ehm

Colour reproduction: Vimnice Printing Press Co. Ltd., Hong Kong.

Printed in China by WKT Co. Ltd.

8206 ISBN: 978-1-905710-21-8

British Library Cataloguing-in-Publication Data.
A catalogue record for this book
is available from the British Library.

If you have enjoyed this book, look out for our
other fun activity books for young children.
Order them from any good bookshop or request a catalogue from:
b small publishing ltd.
The Book Shed, 36 Leyborne Park, Kew, Surrey, TW9 3HA, UK
email: books@bsmall.co.uk
website: www.bsmall.co.uk

b small publishing

Bubble Fun

A bubbly bath is lovely but have you ever wondered how those soapy bubbles are made? This experiment shows you what is happening.

1. Half fill a washbasin with water.

2. Pour a bit of bubble bath into the water.

3. Put a straw into the water and blow!

4

Quick Quizzer!

What's the name of the soap we use to wash our hair?

Let's Take a Closer Look!

When you blow into the water you make loads of bubbles. The bubble bath makes the water elastic, or stretchy, so that it holds the air you are blowing into it. If you blow into water without the bubble bath the water on its own cannot hold the air.

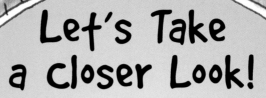

Did You Know?

Your skin never stops growing. When you wash yourself, soap loosens dirt from the skin and also washes away some dead skin. You might find that your fingertips feel smoother after washing your hands!

Always wash your hands after going to the toilet to wash off any germs.

Misty Mirrors

You can do this experiment the next time you have a bath or shower. It'll make getting clean more fun!

1. Shut the bathroom door (but don't lock it!)

2. Run a nice warm bath or shower.

3. Watch what happens to the windows and mirrors in the bathroom.

Let's Take a Closer Look!

The warm bath or shower water gives off a GAS called WATER VAPOUR. This WATER VAPOUR is made when the LIQUID bath water is warmer than the air in the room. When the WATER VAPOUR touches something cold, like a mirror or window, it turns back into LIQUID drops again. This is called CONDENSATION.

Don't leave taps dripping as this wastes water.

Quick Quizzer!

Can you think of another word for water vapour?

Try This!

Breath hard on a cold mirror and see what your warm breath does to it.

7

Beaker Magic

This is a great trick to play on your friends and family. They really won't believe it. Use a plastic beaker just in case you drop it in surprise.

1. Half fill a plastic beaker with water.

2. Put a piece of stiff cardboard over the top of the beaker.

3. Hold the cardboard firmly in place and turn the beaker upside down.

4. Take your hand away from the cardboard.

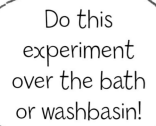

Do this experiment over the bath or washbasin!

Let's Take a Closer Look!

Air all around us is pushing up, down and sideways on everything it touches. This is called AIR PRESSURE. The air pushes up on the cardboard too. It pushes up more strongly than the water and air inside the beaker pushes down. This is why the water does not fall out.

Quick Fact

Air inside your bicycle tyres pushes back too. That's why they can carry your weight as you ride along.

Try This!

Blow up a balloon. If you press your hand against it you can feel the air inside it pushing back.

Float a Boat

How do boats manage to float on the top
of water instead of sinking? In this experiment
you are going to make one and find out.
You need two balls of modelling clay.

1. Make one
ball of clay
into a boat
shape.

2. Fill the
washbasin
with water.

3. Place the
clay ball on
the water.

4. Now place
the clay
boat on the
water.

Let's Take a Closer Look!

The ball of clay sinks to the bottom while the boat FLOATS. The boat stays on the SURFACE of the water because there is air between the sides of it. This makes it light for its size. The ball has no air inside it. It is SOLID and heavy for it size and so it sinks.

Quick Quizzer!

Do you think a toothbrush will sink or float?

Try This!

See if other things in the bathroom float or sink in the water. You could try bottles of shampoo, bars of soap, toothbrushes.

Write or draw which things sink or float in your notebook.

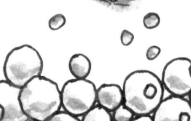

Water Fights Back

You need an empty shampoo or bubble bath bottle for this experiment. You can do it in the bath instead of a washbasin if you like.

1. Put the lid on the bottle. Fill the washbasin with water.

2. Lay the bottle on the top of the water.

3. Let the bottle float on the water.

4. Now try to push the bottle down under the water.

A Greek scientist called Archimedes did experiments like this in his bath too!

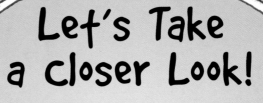

Let's Take a Closer Look!

Like the boat on page 10, the bottle is lighter than the water and so it FLOATS. When you push the bottle down into the water, it is pushing the water out of the way. But the water pushes back and this is why it is difficult to push the bottle down under the water.

Did You Know?

Our bodies are lighter than water so we can float like the bottle. When you are in the sea or the swimming-pool the water is also pushing up against you and helping you to float.

Quick Fact

Deep-sea divers have to wear heavy weights to stop the water pushing them up!

Siphon Fun

Toilets flush because of something called a siphon.
This is what sends the water swooshing round the toilet.
We can make a simple siphon using a long piece of plastic
tube and a large bowl placed next to the washbasin.

1. Half fill the washbasin and put one end of the tube into the water.

2. Suck on the other end until the water is just near your lips.

3. Quickly put your thumb over the end.

4. Hold this end over the bowl and then take your thumb away.

Quick Fact

We use more water in our homes to flush the toilet than for anything else.

Try This!

Make a Water-saver's Chart and get everyone in your house to write down when they've flushed the toilet, had a shower or a bath. Try to make sure no one is wasting water!

Put a towel under the bowl in case you spill any water!

Put your thumb back over the tube to stop the water.

Let's Take a Closer Look!

When you take your thumb away the water flows into the bowl from the washbasin. This is because you have made a SIPHON. AIR PRESSURE on top of the water pushes it into the space you have made when you sucked out the air.

Toothbrush Trick

Light can play some funny tricks on our eyes. This experiment will show you a light trick with a toothbrush.

1. Half fill a clear, plastic beaker with water.

2. Put your toothbrush into the beaker.

3. Have a look at the toothbrush through the sides of the beaker.

Quick Quizzer

Will the toothbrush look bent if you put it in the beaker without water?

Try This!

Next time you go swimming stand in the pool and look down at your legs. They look short and stubby because of refraction.

Let's Take a Closer Look!

The part of the toothbrush under the water looks bent. Light moves more slowly through water than through air. As the light slows down it changes direction and enters your eyes from a different angle. This is why things in water look bent even though they are really straight. It is called REFRACTION.

Don't forget to clean your teeth twice a day!

17

Squirty Squeezers

This experiment will probably spray a lot of water around the place so do it over the bath! You'll need two empty shampoo or bubble bath bottles.

1. Take the caps off the bottles and fill them with water.

2. Put the cap back on to one of the bottles, leaving the lid open.

3. Hold one bottle in each hand and squeeze them both hard!

Did You Know?

A tap has one big hole for the water to come out but a showerhead has lots of small holes in it so that the water shoots out with more power.

Have a towel ready to mop up any water!

Quick Fact

Having a quick shower uses up less water than having a bath.

Let's Take a Closer Look!

When you squeeze the bottles you make the water come out. The bottle with the cap on squirts the water much further. This is because the water is being forced through a much smaller hole than the bottle with the cap off.

Plughole Power

Have you ever watched what happens to the water when you pull the plug out of the bath or basin? This experiment shows you what happens.

1. Put the plug in the washbasin. Fill the basin with water.

2. Float a piece of toilet paper on top of the water.

3. Pull the plug out and watch the toilet paper.

Don't forget to take the toilet paper out of the plughole!

Let's Take a Closer Look!

When you take the plug out of the basin the water does not go straight down the plughole but swirls round. This swirling is called a VORTEX. That is why the toilet paper turns round as the water goes down.

Did You Know?

The Romans did not have toilet paper like us. They used sponges on sticks instead. Yuck!

Quick Quizzer

Why must you wash your hands after using the toilet?

Wrinkly Skin

You might have noticed that when you stay in the bath or a swimming-pool for a long time your hands and feet go all wrinkly. Why is this? (You might like to read a book during this experiment - carefully!)

1. Take a good look at your hands and feet.

2. Run yourself a nice, warm bath.

3. Sit in the water for at least 15 minutes.

4. Have a look at your hands and feet.

Let's Take a Closer Look!

Your fingers and toes have gone all wrinkly. Our skin has some special oil on it to stop water soaking into it. This makes it almost completely WATERPROOF. If you keep your hands and feet in water for ages this oil washes off, your skin soaks up some water and goes all wrinkly.

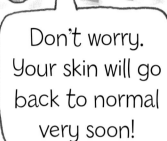

Don't worry. Your skin will go back to normal very soon!

Try This!

Trickle some water on your arm and you will see the water drops run off. They don't soak in because the oil on your skin makes it waterproof.

Quick Fact

You can live for weeks without food but only a few days without water.

23

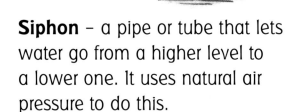

Words to Know

Air Pressure – the force that air places on everything it touches.

Condensation – when a gas changes into a liquid. Water vapour, or steam, changes into drops of water when it touches something cold.

Float – to stay on the top, or surface, of water.

Gas – the air around us is a mixture of different gases. A gas does not have a shape of its own. Water vapour, or steam, is a gas.

Liquid – Water is a liquid. Liquids can be poured and do not have a shape of their own.

Refraction – when light changes direction as it goes into water. This makes you see objects in water in a different way.

Siphon – a pipe or tube that lets water go from a higher level to a lower one. It uses natural air pressure to do this.

Solid – Solid things, like bars of soap and toothbrushes, have a shape of their own.

Surface – the top of something. The surface of water is where it meets the air.

Vortex – water flowing down a plughole makes a whirlpool or vortex. It does not go straight down as lots of water is trying to get down through a small hole.

Water Vapour – the gas that comes off hot or warm water. It is also called steam.

Waterproof – if something is waterproof it does not let water in.

Quizzer Answers

Page 5 – shampoo

Page 7 – steam

Page 11 – it will sink.

Page 17 – no, it will look straight.

Page 21 – to clean off germs.